THANKFULNESS

by Janet McDonnell
illustrated by Linda Hohag
and Lori Jacobson

Created by

THE CHILD'S WORLD

Distributed by CHILDRENS PRESS ®
Chicago, Illinois

CHILDRENS PRESS HARDCOVER EDITION
ISBN 0-516-06309-X

CHILDRENS PRESS PAPERBACK EDITION
ISBN 0-516-46309-8

Library of Congress Cataloging in Publication Data

McDonnell, Janet, 1962-
    Thankfulness / by Janet McDonnell ; illustrated
by Linda Hohag.
        p. cm. — (What is it?)
    Summary: Describes the feeling we call
thankfulness and the things that can make us
thankful.
    ISBN 0-89565-375-3
    1. Gratitude—Juvenile literature.
[1. Gratitude.]   I. Hohag, Linda, ill.   II. Title.
III. Series.
BJ1533.G8M37   1988   88-2657
                                         CIP
                                          AC

© 1988 The Child's World, Inc.
Elgin, IL
All rights reserved. Printed in U.S.A.

1 2 3 4 5 6 7 8 9 10 11 12 R 96 95 94 93 92 91 90 89 88

THANKFULNESS

Glad that I live am I;
That the sky is blue;
Glad for the country lanes,
And the fall of dew.

— Lizette Woodworth Reese
from *A Little Song of Life*

What is thankfulness?

Thankfulness is what you feel when
you have someone to sing you a
song when you can't sleep . . .

and when you have someone to hold
you at the movies during the scary
parts.

You can feel thankful for hot chocolate
and a blanket on a cold, snowy day . . .

or for icy lemonade and a shower on
a hot, dry day.

When you visit your grandma and she has made you your favorite dinner, you feel thankful.

Thankful is how you feel when you slip in the mud and your sister is there to help you up.

You might be thankful for a friend
who shares his brand-new building
blocks . . .

and for a friend who always keeps your secrets.

When it's been raining all morning
and you want to go on a picnic, and
you finally see the sun, you feel
thankful.

And when your mom's flowers are all
dying because the ground is so hard
and dry, you feel thankful when it
finally starts to rain.

You can be thankful for a baby-sitter
who reads all your favorite stories.

And thankful is how you might feel
when your dad finds your favorite car
that you lost a long time ago.

When you have a sore throat and a stuffy nose and your mom brings you ice cream and sits with you, you are thankful.

You can be thankful for big things,
like a park right down the street
where you can play . . .

or for small things, like a chocolate-
chip cookie.

Sometimes you can forget how thankful
you are for something, such as a healthy
body . . .

or a family that loves you.

Thanksgiving Day is a special day that reminds you of all the things you are thankful for.

But if you look very carefully, you
will find something to be thankful for
every day.

Thankfulness is feeling happy for what
you have. When you are thankful, you
feel warm and glad and lucky, all at
the same time.

What are you thankful for today?